Stories in English for Children

English Language for Kids

A Story Book for Kids

English Story and Picture Book for Children Series

English Language and Culture Academy

Table of Contents

The Frog and the Fish

The Frog and the Fish

Once upon a time there was a little frog.

He wanted to catch a fish. He dived and swam after a fish, but unfortunately, the little frog could never catch one.

At some point the little frog got tired and didn't want to chase after the fast fish anymore. So the little frog chose a new game. When there were lots of water and lily leaf floating on the pond, he got the idea of hopping from leave to leave, he wanted to jump from one lily leaf to the other.

But that was not so easy for a little frog with no experience. And it would take courage and strength to do so.

So the little frog first practiced with those leaves lying very close together and near to the pond's edge. Because that way he was sure that he could jump on one and not fall into the water. So he jumped happily from one leaf to the next, he whistled and had fun. The leaves were all close and it was easy.

However, this soon became too boring and too easy for the little frog, and so he chose a leaf that was floating quite far from the shore. He really wanted to jump onto this lily leaf. He was very excited and said to himself: "Yes, I can do it!"

The little frog took a lot of running and made a really big jump.

Then there was a splash, and the little frog fell face down into the water just before he had reached the leaf. The little frog was struggling. A large gulp of water went down his throat, so that he had to cough heavily and could hardly swim. As fast as he could he paddled to the edge of the pond.

His mother was already waiting for him there. She had watched him with a smiling eye: "Come on little one," she said to him lovingly and took him in her arms to comfort him.

"Next time you must be more careful, and you have to practice more, then it will work out."

The little frog listened to his mother. Every day he practiced hopping on water lily leaves. But always in small steps, until one day he could jump on all the

leaves with a very big leap, just like the big frogs do.

Eventually the little frog even caught up with a fish.

The Little Bee

The Little Bee

Once upon a time there was a little bee, and her name was Claire.

Claire was a fast and busy bee. Since it was spring and the flowers were coming out, the little bee was very busy. She had to fly from flower to flower and collect the fine nectar.

This nectar is later turned into delicious honey.

One day, it was a beautiful spring morning, Claire whizzed through the air again. She enjoyed the beautiful weather and the scent of the flowers. She sang:"…all the flowers are already here... !"

Then suddenly, as she was about to fly towards a beautiful, colorful and lush field of flowers, she saw from above a little boy trampling on all the flowers.

He even uprooted some and threw them to the

ground and then trampled on them. Actually the boy

ran into the field and trampled everything onto the

ground and destroyed all the beautiful flowers.

When the little bee Claire saw this, she felt hurt. She

couldn't believe what she saw. The beautiful flowers

had been trampled all over the place!

She had to do something immediately. She flew

straight to the boy, then buzzed around his head.

The boy waved his hands. "Go away you stupid

insect", he said grumpily.

But little bee Claire didn't even think about it,

instead she flew directly on the boy's nose.

She looked him straight in the eyes. "Why are you trampling on the beautiful flowers?" Claire asked him as loudly as she could.

"Don't you know that these little flowers are very important for the nature and for us bees? Are you such an ignorant boy?

The boy was taken aback and rolled his eyes. "Why important? Those are just flowers", he said.

"Don't you know where the honey comes from flowers", the bee asked.

"From the supermarket, of course," the boy said. He was quite sure of himself.

Now the bee Claire had to smile a little.

"Come on, sit down on the grass and let me explain something", she said

The boy sat down on the grass and Claire flew with a slight swing onto a leftover flower that was sticking out of the trampled grass right in front of the boy.

Claire now explained to the boy how the bees suck the nectar out of the flowers. Also the bees add their own juices to the nectar, and at home the bees put the nectar in honeycombs. There it will stay for a while to mature

Then the farmer comes, takes out the honeycomb and throws out the honey. He does that with a machine. And then he can put the honey in jars, and only after that it will be taken to the store or supermarket where you can buy it.

The boy looked down when Claire finished the story. He didn't feel particularly well.

"Then these aren't stupid flowers at all," he murmured.

"These are definitely not stupid flowers," said the bee. "On the contrary, these are useful flowers. For the people and for us bees. We also eat the nectar. If we didn't have it, we would starve. So these are all very good flowers."

"And now I've destroyed them", the boy asked quietly.

Of course, the little bee Claire had already thought about an idea, because she was also a clever bee.

"I need you to do something. Always keep your eyes open and if you see someone trampling or breaking flowers, you go to this person, and tell the story about the bees and the honey. Now you know why flowers are important."

"Yes, I do that!"

"Are you sure?"

"Yes, I will protect the flowers."

"Excellent", clapped the little bee, and took off into the air, flew around the boy's head again, and then she was gone. Because the little bee Claire was also a very busy bee.

The little boy stood still stood there for a while and looked at the sky. Then he waved:

"Bye, bye you little clever bee."

The Fox and his Friends

The Fox and his Friends

Once upon a time there was a little fox who lived with his family in the middle of a big forest. Of course, many other animals also lived there. There were hedgehogs, wild boars, owls, deer, beetles and other animals. Behind the forest was a meadow with cows. Frenchy the little fox had many friends. He not only played with his siblings, but was also friends with Tony the hedgehog and Hugo the wild boar. His best friend to this day is Emma the goose.

Summer was his favorite season. It was nice, there was enough to eat and he could swim in the little pond in front of the meadow. Frenchy really enjoyed it. Sometimes, when he could gather all his courage, he would run quickly between the cows. A bit behind the meadow lives another friend of his - Elsa the chicken. But unfortunately, Elsa is never allowed to come out to play. She lives behind a high fence and Frenchy always tells her the best stories.

In winter it is also nice in the forest. The friends can search for tracks and hide in the snow. And if the frost is really strong they'd skate on the frozen pond. This always looks very funny because Frenchy can perform many tricks on the ice. Of course he also goes to visit his girlfriend Elsa the chicken in winter. In winter he doesn't have to run across the meadow, because the cows are all in the barn because it's much too cold for them outside.

On one such winter day, Frenchy was sitting on a big snow-covered tree stump with his brother Beansy and sister Lola. They drew things in the snow and Lola built a snowman. Suddenly Frenchy looked up. "Can you hear that?"

Now his siblings also became aware of that sound. Frenchy turned his head to point his ear in the right direction. There - again. Beansy shrugged, but Lola asked: "Is that Elsa?"

Suddenly, a loud and excited cackle was heard.

All three ran. The little fox had never run across the meadow so fast in his entire life. He ran and ran. Breathless, he stopped in front of the high fence. Behind them, Elsa flapped her wings wildly. She cackled loudly and paced back and forth like she was afraid of something. And then they saw it. A strange fox was actually tampering with the fence.

"Hey you", Frenchy shouted. "You better get out of here and leave my girlfriend alone."

"Get out of here now," Lola shouted. Together with his siblings and with all his courage, the little fox saved the chicken's life. That was the beginning of a true friendship.

The Rescue of the Baby Owl

The Rescue of the Baby Owl

Not long ago there was a famous little red fox who was just called Frenchy. Why is our buddy, the fox, called Frenchy? All the animals say it is because he originally came from a different place, a different forest. Although no one could tell where exactly Frenchy came from, he has always lived with us.

Everyone, including children, know Frenchy as a lucky, good fox they can rely on. Actually, Frenchy has a secret bond with the children from the village.

Interestingly and as a matter of fact, Frenchy the fox was not always the strong, quick, and lucky fox he is today. When Frenchy was still very small and still went to the forest school, things were quite different.

Most of the other animals in school knew nothing about Frenchy the fox. Frenchy was often teased by his classmates because he was still so small and weak, and he couldn't run as fast and jump as high as the others. Even if he tried and practiced, his short little legs just couldn't get any faster or higher.

To avoid being ridiculed by other animals too often, Frenchy often stayed alone. At closing time, he would go out alone and go home alone. One day, while strolling around, Frenchy encountered a large group of animals that had gathered around a small area where there were no trees. He couldn't see the animals until he got closer to them. Then the big mother owl recognized him and cried: "Frenchy, come here! My baby owl fell out of the nest and plummeted straight into this deep hole. Now it's stuck there and can't get out anymore, and all the other animals in the forest are too big to climb into the hole to save my baby. Can you please help me?"

Frenchy didn't think twice and crawled into the hole where the little owl was trapped. When he reached the baby owl, he carefully grabbed his plumage with his pointed teeth and crawled backward out of the hole, keeping the baby owl in his mouth. When Frenchy finally made it out, all the animals cheered and clapped and were happy about the rescue of the baby owl. The mother owl thanked Frenchy and invited him to play with her children.

The rescue operation by Frenchy is still known among all the animals in the forest today.

And since that day, the other animals decided not to tease Frenchy anymore as he taught them that both young and old animals can do great things.

Easter Eggs

Easter Eggs

Rosa's class teacher has hidden a lot of eggs outside the school building in the nearby woods. Today is Easter and whoever finds the most eggs gets a special Easter surprise, Mr. Jones, the school director said.

Rosa is excited. She is searching for the eggs with her friends Tony, Benny and Marta. But unfortunately, they haven't found more than two eggs so far.

"We don't win like that!" Rosa says, getting slightly annoyed and points to the other classmates. Some already have four or more eggs in their baskets.

"It doesn't matter," says Tony good-naturedly. "Eggs actually have nothing in common with Easter."

"I know. But I still want to win."

Rosa keeps her eyes on the floor, considering Tony's words. Maybe he's right after all. At Easter they celebrate the resurrection of Jesus Christ, who died for their sins. Suddenly Rosa has an idea.

She says: "At Easter, one should not look down to the ground, but up to the sky."

Tony starts talking about Easter traditions, but Rosa doesn't listen. "That's it", she says. "The eggs might be hidden all up there in the tree!"

She looks up and actually sees something colorful flashing on the branches just about eight feet above the ground.

A minute later she's already climbed up to the branch with a basket in her hand. She finds five colorful eggs! So she definitely has won the search game.

Her classmates look at her in astonishment. Even Mr. Jones smiles.

"Hey all of you!" Rosa shouts. "You should look up instead of looking down. Especially at Easter!"

Where is our Cat?

Where Is Our Cat?

One morning we found a dead bird lying in front of our door. It looked like someone placed it there.

I told my mother: "I think our cat Mika did this."

My mother answered: "That's nature, we must not interfere."

I disagreed. "That's dangerous."

"Why?"

"The dead bird carries bacteria. Mika will bring the bacteria into our house."

"You are right", said my mother concerned.

My mother had to make a decision.

She took the cat into the house.

After that I never saw Mika again.

School Starts Soon

If you practice something really well, then it works!"

Grandfather always said that when something didn't work out right away. And he was right about that. The child had already been able to learn a lot. Not right away, but after hard practice. Like walking backwards, swimming, riding a bike, fishing, and playing the guitar, all very important things that required a lot of practice.

"Practice makes perfect!" the grandfather often said when the child came to visit him.

But soon there would be many new things to learn, because after the summer holidays the child would go to school for the first time.

The child was a little worried. Who are the teachers? And was there anyone who knew more than grandfather? The child could not really believe it. No one in the world was smarter than him. You could learn anything from him.

And because this was a fact, the child actually had little desire to go to school. It was also afraid of the first day in school and all the strangers the child would meet there. He would like to stay with his grandfather in the village forever and learn everything he taught him. With him, he didn't need to be afraid.

"I only want to learn from you!" said the child to the grandfather. "You are the best teacher. I don't need the others."

Grandfather didn't answer right away. He looked at the child for a long time.

"So you're scared too," he finally said.

Why, was grandfather also scared? No, a grandfather wasn't afraid of nothing and nobody.

"You're never afraid," said the child. "And you don't have to go to school either."

"Because I learned it," answered the grandfather.

"Like what?"

"The thing about school and the fears."

"Can I learn not to be afraid?" The child was amazed. "Can I really do that?"

The grandfather nodded. "You can learn anything you want to learn. And we will practice that with the fears. "

And that's what they did until the end of the holidays. They practiced not being afraid and looking forward to school and the teachers and the many new classmates.

The Monster in the Basement

The Monster in the Basement

"Tony, will you go into the basement and bring up potatoes?" asked the grandmother. "I'll make it your favorite dish, pancakes" she promised.

Tony didn't like grandma's cellar. That little window there barely lit up the room, even when the sun was shining outside. He found it very creepy. He took the basket, went down the stairs and stopped just outside the door.

As he cautiously opened it, that door squeaked louder and more eerily than ever. Before taking a step into the dark room, he dipped his hand in and felt for the light switch on the wall to the right. The light went on, illuminating only the center of the room, but all corners of the great basement remained hidden in darkness. He quickly walked through and grabbed the stored potatoes.

Suddenly the door slammed behind him. He started and held his breath.

He heard a noise, it came from the darkest corner behind him.

He turned around carefully. Luminous pairs of eyes looked at him and slowly moved towards him.

He dropped everything, ran to the door, yanked it open, quickly shut it behind him and ran up the stairs screaming: "Granny!" he called out breathlessly, his heart pounding in his throat.

"Downstairs... In the basement... A monster!"

Grandma went down to the basement, Tony followed her from a safe distance.

She opened the door.

"Tony, come to me, I discovered your monster", she laughed with all her heart.

An animal, black as night, brushed against Grandma's legs.

It was Marle the cat. And, the door that slammed behind Tony was caused by a draft, which sometimes happens when doors or windows are open and the wind blows in from outside. Tony understood it now and hasn't been afraid to go down into the basement ever since.

The Birthday Child

The Birthday Child

The sun was shining and the weather was really lovely. There couldn't be a better day for a small birthday party. But the little birthday boy is still sleeping peacefully in his bed.

The sun squinted through the drawn curtain. It tickled little Paul's nose and he had to sneeze. Just five minutes later, Paul was sitting up in his bed. He knew very well that today was a special day. Excitedly he threw the blanket aside and ran down to the kitchen, where his mother was already waiting for him. But what was going on here? Where were all the nice presents? There wasn't even a cake on the table. Had Paul's mother really forgotten him?

Little Paul didn't understand that, his mother had never forgotten him. Every morning he had a big birthday cake on the table and his presents next to it. He was a little sad, but sat down at the kitchen table without saying a word. Maybe he was wrong and today wasn't even the 4th of July.

When his mother still didn't turn around to him after another 10 minutes and at least congratulated him, Paul got up and tugged at his mother's sleeve. She was startled and turned around abruptly. Her other sleeve got caught in the bread machine and her shirt tore in two. Paul's mother was upset, but that wasn't his intention. He just wanted to be noticed.

Disappointed, Paul went to school with no breakfast and no gifts. He arrived at school full of hope.

Maybe at least his friends hadn't forgotten his birthday. But his hopes were in vain. Nobody came up to him and congratulated him. Paul was beginning to doubt himself. After a terrible day at school Paul went home again. He also didn't feel like celebrating his birthday anymore, and everyone had forgotten about it.

When he opened the front door and wanted to enter, suddenly a lot of people yelled "surprise". Paul didn't even know what happened to him until he saw the mess. So his mother and friends hadn't forgotten him after all, and he wasn't wrong either. So today was indeed his birthday. They weren't allowed to say anything because his mother had thrown a surprise party. Now he understood everything.

It was a great party, and he received many presents. He also blew out the candles on his beautiful birthday cake and wished he never had to go through anything like that again. In the end, his mother even organized a birthday clown for him. Paul was over the moon, just enjoying the afternoon with his friends and family. And when everyone had left, he asked his mother why she had kept everything a secret from him. His mother laughed and replied that she just wanted to give him a surprise and that it finally succeeded. Satisfied and with a smile on his face, Paul went to his bed and promptly fell asleep.

Traffic and Kids

Traffic and Kids

Our son is already six years old. It's time that he learns some of the traffic rules since he loves riding his bicycle through the neighborhood. We tell him, if he crosses a street he must look to his right side first. Then he must check his left side, and only when no cars are coming is he allowed to cross the street. Especially when he sees a stop sign or a traffic light he must be very careful. If he sees a red light for pedestrians, he must stop and wait until it turns green. Some areas even have a few bicycle lanes which is kind of new to us, but even with those lanes, kids must be careful to use them and never speed!

The Circus

The Circus

Today I went with my mother to the circus. The show started at six, but we arrived early because we knew there would be a long line at the ticket box. My mother asked why the tickets are so expensive. The salesperson explained that they have big animals such as tigers and lions, and they need to eat enormous amounts of meat every day.

Finally, the show starts. First we see a clown who makes jokes by gesturing with his hands. Then a huge cage is set up and the animals arrive. We see an elephant that raises a leg, a monkey that is dressed in a girly school costume, and then we see the big cats led into the cage. A tiger has to jump through a burning ring, and a lion has to jump from stool to stool. I ask my mother if the animals are also doing such things in nature. My mother responds that she doesn't know.

The Polluted Lake

The Polluted Lake

Marie and Luke went on a trip to the lake with their parents, but when they got there, they were very scared because the whole lake was full of rubbish. Plastic bags were floating everywhere and the water was brown in color. But the worst was the water smelled like rotten eggs.

The mother said: "Then is no swimming today. We're going to have a picnic though."

After the meal the children played on the bank. They found that there was a particularly large amount of garbage on one side of the lake. Curious, Marie and Luke circled the body of water and found a small stream on the other side that emptied into the lake.

The water in the creek looked even worse than that in the lake, with bags, packaging and other rubbish floating in the water everywhere.

"Where does all this junk come from?" Luke asked.

"We could follow the creek and see if we can find a clue," Marie suggested.

They walked along the creek. The further they went, the thicker the carpet of garbage on the water became. The amount of garbage almost made Luke cry. He said: "We can't just leave the rubbish in the water!"

Marie objected, "It's way too much to fish it all out!"

"We still have to try!" Luke contradicted indignantly. He found a long stick and began fishing plastic bags and other debris out of the water. After a while, Marie also picked up a stick from the ground and helped him. However, Luke soon realized that their hard work made little difference.

Seeing his disappointment, Marie said: "Come on, let's go a little further. If we can figure out how the garbage gets into the creek, maybe we can make a bigger difference."

The children went on. A large gray building suddenly appeared behind a clump of trees, with a thick pipe sticking out of the wall.

Luke pointed to it and whispered to Marie, "Look, that's where all the junk is coming out!"

Marie nodded. The two children sorted around the building and found a door. Inside they found a huge hall with conveyor belts. Little devils stood on each conveyor belt and tore up garbage that was transported outside into the river.

"You have to stop this immediately!" Marie commanded loudly.

The devils were startled when they saw the children, but they kept throwing the trash onto the conveyor belts. Thankfully, Luke had an idea.

"Devils don't like pretty things," he said. "Let's sing a beautiful song about the sunshine and the flowers."

As soon as they started singing, the little devils clapped their hands over their ears and wailed: "Stop it! Stop!"

"We won't stop until you stop polluting the water," Marie said.

"Okay, okay," the little devils murmured.

"And you also have to collect the garbage from the creek and the lake again," Luke demanded.

"Never!" cried the devils. But after Marie and Luke sang another beautiful song for a few minutes, the little devils gave in and promised to clean everything up. Satisfied, the children returned to their parents - and when they came back to the lake a week later, it was actually clean.

"Now we have to make sure the water stays that way," they told themselves. "Because if we throw garbage in it ourselves, it's just as bad as if the devils do it."

Food Poisoning

Food Poisoning

My brother Marco feels terrible; he's been in bed since yesterday. He has nausea, a headache, coughing and diarrhea. He also feels extremely exhausted and tired. My father drives my brother to the doctor. He explains the conditions to the doctor and the doctor examines Marco.

The doctor finds out that Marco has food poisoning. It's a dangerous situation, because Marco is already dehydrated! The doctor also prescribes that Marco stay in bed and take strong medication twice a day. My brother believes his food poisoning comes from a kebab he had eaten the day before when he stopped downtown.

She Loves to Help

She Loves to Help

Mimi is nine years old. From Monday to Friday, she goes to school, and around one o' clock she takes the bus home. Usually the bus is crowded with other students. Sometimes the elderly take the bus too, as many of them are just too old to drive a car. Mimi is a kind and compassionate young girl. If she sees an elderly person riding on the bus, she offers her seat, because for older people it can be very hard to stand on a moving bus. At the bus station, there is a traffic light for pedestrians. It has a new system where one has to push a button to get a green light. Many elderly have trouble with this and Mimi never hesitates to help old people to cross the street. Mimi already has an idea on what she wants to do in the future; she thinks it would be a very rewarding work

if she could become a professional caretaker.

Ticket Control

Ticket Control

I remember when I was a kid I spent some time in the north of the country; I even went to school there. In this area, trains are part of daily transportation. Actually, I like trains more than buses. We were a group of four children and it was winter with a lot of snow. Laura was one of the smaller children, at that time she was only nine years old. We made a trip by train from one city to another city. It was a nice and modern train, and we had even our own compartment. We heard somebody knocking on the door. It was the ticket inspector, a man in uniform, he needed to check if we had bought our tickets. One by one he inspected the tickets, but Laura was nervously searching her bag; she couldn't find her ticket. The inspector asked for her identification, then told her to follow him. At that time the train had stopped in a small town. We waited for Laura to return but nothing happened. Suddenly the train moved and through the window we could see Laura standing by herself at the train station. But Laura looked different. She looked very scared. Then we noticed that Laura was just standing there without her jacket! She had left it here, and apparently the inspector had kicked her off the train, letting her freezing at the train station. Days later we found out, she took the next train to the city.

Swimming

Swimming

We are a group of boys and are avid swimmers. Most of us are ten years old, and only our friend Peter is eight.

Every Friday afternoon we go to the public swimming pool. First, we need to go to the locker rooms. There we change our clothing to proper swimwear, and after that we'll take a shower. Before and after swimming one has to take a shower, which is obligatory in public swimming pools. Sometimes taking a shower takes quite some time, because we like to make jokes and are fooling around. Once in the swimming pool, we jump from the plank and swim around. We start with 200 meters breaststroke, after that, we usually go on to twenty minutes of freestyle. Towards the end we just play water ball. At the edge of the pool a lifeguard is always there observing us.

Last week when we were finished swimming, we didn't shower afterwards because an unknown child had left his excrements in the shower.

My Hobbies

My name is Miriam and I have many hobbies. The reason is simple; I just have many different interests.

As a kid I had a large doll collection, but now my likes have changed. Nowadays I am very much interested in art. I like to paint and I am especially fond of reading books. Actually, I read all kind of nonfiction books, even history. I also like to play the piano. Music is one of my favorite pastimes. Being involved with many hobbies is actually a tradition in our family. My sister likes to read books about philosophy and everyone in my family participates in cultural activities. Besides reading and music, I also like to play tennis and on special occasions, such as on vacation, I like to play golf. My parents are much more into animal breeding. My father is an expert with dogs and exotic animals. If time allows, I love to travel. However, I consider myself more of an explorer than a typical tourist. Having many hobbies and doing a lot of sports keeps my mind and body active, and helps me to look forward in life as well.

School and our Future Plans

Sabine goes to school. Her teacher would like to know what the students want to do in the future as a profession.

"What profession would you all like to have in the future?" asks the teacher.

Micheal is the first to raise his hand. "I'd like to become a doctor, so I can cut open bodies and see what's in there."

Lukas nods and raises his hand. "I want to become a police officer, so I can shoot the bad guys."

Nicole is laughing as she goes next. "I would like to become a pilot, then I can feel as free as a bird."

Finally it's Sabine's turn. "I want to become a teacher. I would like to help students be able to make good decisions about what they want to become in the future."

***